Gillen

This booklet was written by Darren Gillen, Research Analyst at GillenMarkets, and is also available in eBook format (PDF, ePub or Kindle).

About Gillen

Gillen is a boutique investment advisor offering expert advice on the management of personal, pension and corporate monies. We place a strong emphasis on fully understanding our clients' needs, so that we can make informed decisions and plans, together.

We are investment advisors, not product sellers. Our investment solutions are structured to meet the specific needs of each individual client with minimum assets of €500k.

Our investment advisory fee structure aligns our interests with yours, ensuring that we sit on the same side of the table as our clients.

With our fee structure, there are:

- No upfront commissions or fees payable by clients.

- No dealing costs.

- No early redemption penalties.

- No VAT.

Just a transparent 1.0% annual advisory fee on the assets under advice.

We also offer a subscription-based investment newsletter for do-it-yourself investors and training courses both in-person and online for those wishing to learn more about the principles of sound investing.

We believe trust is earned. Our belief is that we work for clients, looking at each individual's needs and taking a commonsense, long-term approach.

We have built an outstanding team with the depth of knowledge and experience to meet all our clients' investment needs. We have an appetite for learning and sharing and we always partner with our clients as equals.

We'd like to hear from you!

Contact details

T: + 353 (0)1 287 1400
E: info@gillenmarkets.com
W: www.gillenmarkets.com

Follow us on Facebook, LinkedIn, Twitter and Gillenmarkets.com.

ILTB Ltd (trading as Gillen/GillenMarkets) is regulated by the Central Bank of Ireland.

Bricks & Mortar through Stocks & Shares

Property Investing in the Stock Markets

A **GillenMarkets** Publication

Darren Gillen

Published by Oak Tree Press, Cork T12 XY2N
www.oaktreepress.com / www.SuccessStore.com

© 2023 ILTB Ltd t/a GillenMarkets

A catalogue record of this book is available from the British Library.

ISBN 978 1 78119 579 6 (Paperback)
ISBN 978 1 78119 580 2 (PDF)
ISBN 978 1 78119 581 9 (ePub)
ISBN 978 1 78119 582 6 (Kindle)

Disclaimer
Investing carries risk and none of the stocks or funds highlighted in this booklet constitute a recommendation by the author, GillenMarkets or the publisher and none of these parties can assume liability for any losses that may be sustained should a reader subsequently invest in them, and any such liability is hereby disclaimed. Readers should take professional advice before making any investment. None of the material in this publication constitutes investment advice or an offer to invest in any of the funds referred to. No one receiving this publication should treat it as a personal recommendation as it does not take into account the needs and objectives, personal circumstances, including investment experience, financial position, or attitude to risk of recipients.
Warning
Past performance is not a reliable guide to future performance.

CONTENTS

Gillen.

Other Publications from GillenMarkets

3 STEPS TO INVESTMENT SUCCESS (2012)
How to Obtain the Returns While Controlling the Risk
Rory Gillen

A PATH TO FINANCIAL FREEDOM (2nd edition / 2023)
A Guide to Sound Investing
Rory Gillen

TIMING THE MARKETS (2023)
Unemotional Approaches to Making Buy & Sell Decisions in Markets
Rory Gillen

PRIVATE EQUITY: ACCESS FOR ALL (2023)
Investing in Private Equity through the Stock Markets
Jonathan Yates

INTELLIGENT GOLD INVESTING (2nd edition / 2023)
Including a Section on Bitcoin
Rory Gillen

UNDERSTANDING ALTERNATIVE ASSETS (2nd edition / 2023)
Gold, Forestry, Government & Corporate Bonds, Renewable Energy &
Hedge Strategies
Rory Gillen

All available in print and ebook formats from
GillenMarkets.com, SuccessStore.com & Amazon

SUMMARY

Property is often the favoured asset class for investors looking to earn attractive returns on their savings. This is particularly true in Ireland. And the most popular way to do this – despite the lessons offered by our property and financial crises that in Ireland lasted from 2008 to end 2012 – is to invest directly into a (usually, residential) property. The reason for this, we suspect, is due to a perception among Irish investors that investing directly into property is a less risky undertaking than most others – such as investing in property through the stock market or investment funds.

This perception is, quite simply, incorrect. Our aim is to improve your understanding of what constitutes sound property investing and the choices you have in that regard.

You will, for a start, be able to explain the general characteristics of property investing and list the different types of property available for investment.

You will learn about the historical returns generated by commercial properties in Ireland. Furthermore, you will be able to explain exactly how those returns were generated. Terms like 'rental yield' will enter your lexicon, and you will have a clearer understanding of how and why rental incomes tend to grow in line with society's prosperity.

Interest rates act like gravity in finance – lower interest rates lead to rising asset prices, and higher interest rates lead to falling asset prices. By the end of this booklet, you will understand exactly why that is, and therefore why interest rates are a key driver of property returns in the short- to medium-term (although interest rate movements have much less influence over the long-term). Wow (or bore) your friends in the pub with your knowledge of investing arcana!

Having established the fundamentals, we can then deal with the contentious claim made above: investing in physical property is *not* less risky than investing in property through stock markets or funds. We introduce the concepts of location risks, financial risks, and valuation risks. You will see that these risks are the same whether investing directly in property or *via* funds or stocks. Indeed, these risks are often better controlled when done through the stock market or funds.

We provide an instructive example of two investors – one who builds a portfolio slowly over time through a listed property fund, while the other buys a direct property at a single point in time. You will see the advantages of regular investing in the stock market, and how it can control the key risks all investors face with investing. You will see, further, the disaster that was wreaked on people's savings (and lives) when they invested in a single overvalued property using debt – the consequences are long-lasting and painful.

Our aim is not to argue against direct property investing. It is a perfectly sound endeavour when undertaken in a prudent, risk-controlled manner. Nonetheless, misconceptions abound. We hope that this book will give you a deeper, more nuanced understanding of how property investing works. This, in turn, will hopefully increase the odds of you earning attractive investment returns.

After all, the sharpened pencil writes the clearest prose. Happy reading.

Darren Gillen
March 2023

INTRODUCTION

This booklet is aimed at the person who is interested in learning about the various ways to save and invest in property over one's lifetime.

The sole purpose of property investing is to earn a return on one's surplus capital (savings) – and preferably a return that exceeds the risk-free returns available from assets like bank deposits. Property, like equities, is a risk asset, and thus investors should earn a premium return for the risks involved (referred to as the risk premium) over time. In the case of property, returns are earned from both rental income and growth in capital values over the medium- to long-term. Interest rates also play a role in property prices, as we shall demonstrate.

Buying a house or an apartment is probably the most common way for investors to gain access to property. This is understandable: being of bricks and mortar makes the investment very tangible, and also comes without the key drawback (and opportunity) of listed companies – a daily quoted price.

However, there are some key drawbacks associated with a direct property purchase: you can't buy a brick at a time, and you have to buy all the bricks in one place, in one go and probably with the use of some debt. In other words, a direct property investor buys a single property (location risk), probably using debt (financial risk), and at a single point in time (valuation risk).

Despite the perception that direct property investing is an attractive way to use one's savings, it is our view that this activity is riskier than many appreciate.

Saving and investing *via* property funds – available in Ireland from a number of life companies, or on the stock markets, offers significant advantages. A property fund or stock offers diversification, no need for personal debt, and allows the investor to build a property portfolio 'brick-by-brick' by investing a small sum of capital on a regular basis. The investor also benefits from professional managers, who know how to appraise property values and manage a portfolio, as well as dealing with the day-to-day issues that arise – no more calls from tenants in the middle of the night that the washing machine flooded the apartment!

It is more important than ever to be informed about the risks of property investing. An investor must be sure that she understands the key drivers of property returns, how property prices today compare to history and to incomes in society, and how interest rates impact the value of a property. Against a backdrop of high inflation and rising interest rates, this latter point has become particularly pertinent.

It is our view that sensible investing leads to attractive returns, and sensible investing begins with understanding the risks that you are taking. Once you understand the risks, you can decide whether the likely return on offer is suitable compensation. We hope that this booklet serves as a reliable guide in that regard.

1: AN INTRODUCTION TO PROPERTY

THE GENERAL CHARACTERISTICS OF PROPERTY INVESTING

Rent on a commercial or residential property is a fixed cost and is generally negotiated on a medium- to long-term basis (medium- to long-term leases). Leases generally have periodic adjustments upwards (and downwards), so that rental income streams also can be adjusted upwards over time for inflation, although they can also decline in recessionary conditions. Nonetheless, these defensive characteristics of physical property are attractive compared to the greater cyclicality that characterises corporate earnings and equity markets.

The long-term drivers of property returns are more or less the same as for general equities. The initial rental yield plus the growth in the rental income largely determines an investor's total return from property over time. In equities, it is the initial dividend yield plus the growth in the dividend income stream that largely determines the total returns to an equity investor over time.

In the case of property, the growth in rental income is normally reflected in capital appreciation of the property. For equities, the growth in the dividend income is normally reflected in the growth in the share price (capital growth) over time.

Declining interest rates, as was the case in the developed world from 1982 to 2021, make the rental yield and dividend yield and their likely future growth more attractive to an investor, so that lower interest rates can further boost the capital values of property and business (equities). The corollary, of course, is also true: rising interest rates can act as a drag on capital values for both property and equities. We will explore this idea in detail in a later section.

Whereas the returns on capital in industry (business) are generally higher than in property, sensible use of leverage (borrowings) can boost the normal returns available from property and without much additional risk.

Good quality businesses, though, will always have the edge given that they have the ability to reinvest their earnings at high rates of return, which fuels faster growth. In property investing, this growth opportunity does not really exist. You can't reinvest in an existing property, aside from once-off upgrades or refurbishments.

THE MAIN PROPERTY TYPES

Broadly speaking, property investments can be broken down into two segments: residential and commercial property.

Residential

Residential properties are the first category of investable property assets. Investors in this area can purchase either individual properties (single-family homes) or apartment blocks (multi-family homes). Individual investors are likely, if they make a direct property investment, to invest in a single house or apartment, while institutional investors are more likely to invest in multi-family units (blocks of apartments) given the larger amounts of capital at their disposal.

Commercial

Commercial property includes any property which permits a business to engage in economic activity. The main sub-segments of commercial property include:

- Offices.
- Retail – supermarkets, shopping centres, retail stores.
- Industrial & logistics – warehouses, factories, distribution centres.
- Leisure – hotels, pubs, restaurants, cafés, sports facilities.
- Healthcare – hospitals, medical centres, nursing homes.

Emerging & Alternative Property Types

Finally, we include here certain property asset classes which don't fit easily into the above categorisations, or which are relatively new and beginning to attract institutional interest and professionalisation. These segments primarily include:

- Student accommodation;
- Self-storage facilities.

THE IRISH RESIDENTIAL & COMMERCIAL PROPERTY MARKET

Irish Residential Property

Residential property or multifamily apartment complexes have often been described as being more defensive than other property investments. During a downturn, office or retail properties may be vacated, but it is less likely residential property will be vacated.

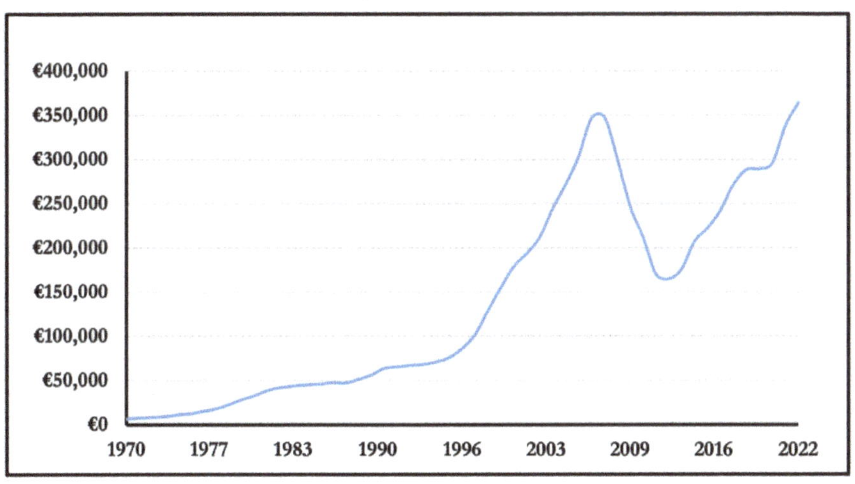

Chart 1: Irish Residential Property Prices

Source: CSO, Department of Housing, Local Government & Heritage.

Chart 1 shows the evolution of Irish residential property prices since 1970. It shows the average property price for both houses and apartments across all regions.

Irish residential property prices have risen steadily across time, but the most noticeable feature of the chart is, of course, the acceleration in prices during the property boom of the early- to mid-2000s. Between 1996 and 2006, property prices increased 301%. Returns were double-digit in all of those years except two – and in those two years, the gains were over 8%.

The property market reached a peak in April 2007, after which it continued to fall for almost six years. Overall, it fell 55% to a trough in March 2013.

Recovery in the Irish economy, and a fall in property prices so that they were once more in line with incomes, meant that property prices could begin to recover. Since March 2013, property prices have risen 130% (8.9% annualised), and only surpassed the April 2007 peak in July 2022 – over 15 years after the property bubble burst. Such is the damage that can be wrought by speculative excess.

Some areas of the market have still not fully recovered. Dublin apartments, for example, remain 18% below the peak in February 2007.

Chart 2: Dublin Prime Residential Yield *vs* 10-year Government Bond

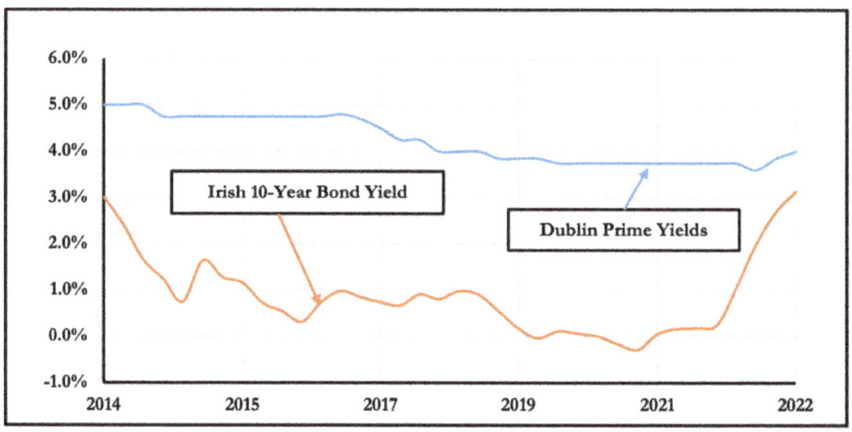

Source: CBRE & Bloomberg.

Chart 2 highlights the net prime residential 'Build to Rent' yield on multifamily investment opportunities in Dublin. (Build to Rent means private residential property which is designed for rental services rather than sale.)

Our data source for residential yields is from CBRE and only dates back to 2014 as 'Build to Rent' investment did not exist in the Irish market until that date. We focus on Dublin as it is the most developed residential market in

Ireland. The net prime residential yield is the yield for the owner of the property on the lease to a tenant, adjusted to reflect purchasing costs and ongoing charges such as maintenance.

As we can see from the chart, the prime residential yield has declined from 5.0% in 2014 to a low of 3.6% during 2022, reflecting strong investor demand over the period. Attractive starting yields, a growing economy, and falling interest rates set the stage for good property returns over the subsequent decade. For example, IRES REIT, a significant investor in (mostly) Dublin apartments, generated 10.7% annualised net asset value (NAV) growth since listing in 2014, albeit a portion of the return was due to the trust's use of debt.

Looking to the future, the Irish residential property market – particularly Dublin – faces both tailwinds and headwinds. Opportunities include population growth, increasing urbanisation in the major cities, a strong economy and labour market, and foreign direct investment from multinationals. Further, favourable demand-supply dynamics (less houses are being built than needed) and the affordability of mortgages over renting are supportive of house prices.

Risks include rising interest rates, which impact both rental income (where financed by debt) and asset prices, low growth potential in rents due to rental caps, and higher house prices in Dublin. A more detailed discussion of the risks and opportunities in Dublin residential property is found in our Irish Residential Properties REIT research note, available to subscribers on our website.

Irish Commercial Property

Chart 3 shows the progression of average rents per square metre for prime office property located in Dublin. We take offices as a proxy for the commercial market, with office properties accounting for *circa* 70% to 75% of investment capital in Irish commercial property.

The movements in Dublin office rents highlight the boom and bust of the mid-2000s, as well as the subsequent recovery.

Between 1989 and the peak in March 2007, Dublin prime office rents increased 228%, from €205 per square metre to €673 per square metre, an annualised growth rate of 7.1%. Inflation over the same period grew at a slower 3.0% annualised (67% cumulative).

The subsequent deep recession in Ireland saw office rents fall 56% from peak to trough, a process which took five years to complete and saw rents bottom at €296 per square metre in early 2012. We took a positive view on Irish commercial property in mid-2013, highlighting that attractive starting yields (office property traded at a yield of 6.5% to 7.0%), a recovering economy, recovering rental incomes, and falling bond yields (*i.e.*, interest rates) all pointed to attractive returns from Irish commercial property going forward.

Chart 3: Prime Dublin Office Rents (per metre sq. *p.a.*)

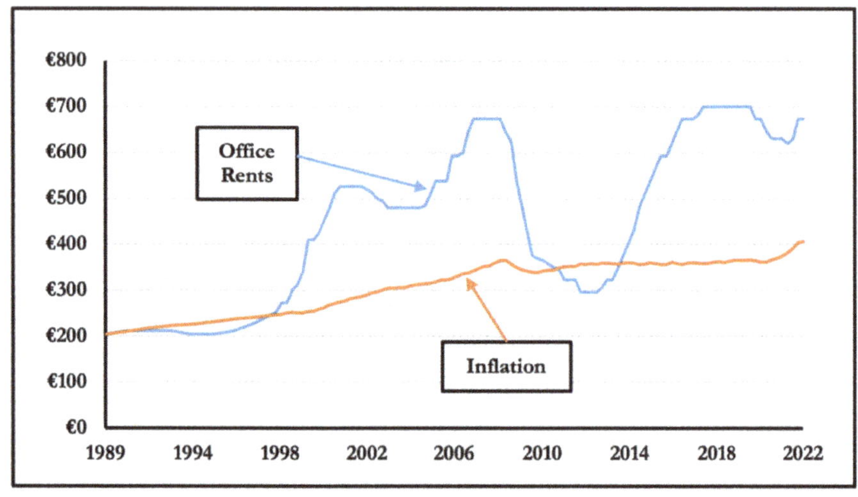

Source: CBRE & CSO.

From the bottom in March 2012, Dublin prime office rents have grown 127% (8.1% annualised) to €673 per square metre. Current rents are slightly below the all-time peak (€700 per square metre), reflecting the damage wrought by the Covid-19 pandemic.

THE LINK BETWEEN INCOME & PROPERTY PRICES

One of the key drivers of residential property prices is the level of incomes in society. Increasing incomes mean, all else being equal, that housing becomes increasingly affordable. We would expect, therefore, that property prices would increase in line with *per capita* incomes in society.

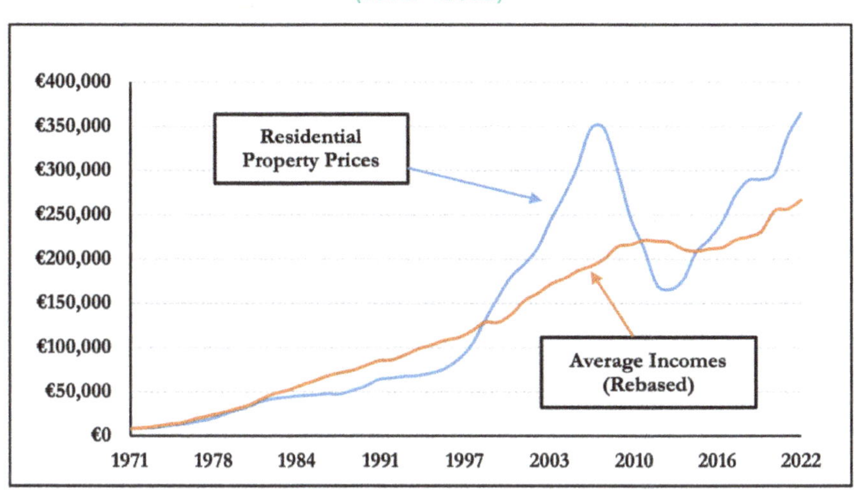

Chart 4: Irish Residential Property Prices *vs* Average Annual Income
(1971 – 2022)

Source: CSO, Department of Housing, Local Government & Heritage.

Chart 4 confirms this intuition. It shows Irish residential property prices and average annual income *per capita* from 1971-2022. Average annual incomes have been rebased to the 1971 property prices to aid comparison. As we can see, Irish property prices have tracked society's incomes over the long-term – although property prices have been much more volatile, with significant price increases between 1997-2007 and significant price declines between 2007-2012. Incomes, on the other hand, have been more stable, with the only (more modest) decline occurring during the Global Financial Crisis period.

In 1971, the average house in Ireland cost €7,900 and average annual income per person employed was €1,700, so that house prices were *circa* 4.6 times income. Today, the average house price is €364,500 and average annual income per person employed is €57,900, so that house prices today are *circa* 6.3 times incomes – *i.e.,* residential property has become increasingly expensive. The average ratio of house prices to incomes has been 4.7 since 1970.

(A note on data: The income figures we use are taken from Ireland's national accounts and, in addition to basic wages and salaries, include items such as overtime, bonuses, commissions, and other income. The house price series is an average and can be skewed upwards by expensive properties. The median property price was €330,000 at the end of December 2022.)

The increase in the ratio likely reflects both falling interest rates (which makes mortgages more affordable and thus pushes up demand for residential property), more households having two incomes (*i.e.*, more women participate in the workforce compared to earlier years), and a chronic lack of housing supply in Ireland.

In general, however, the key point holds: property prices track *per capita* incomes over long periods of time.

2: THE HISTORICAL RETURNS FROM COMMERCIAL PROPERTY INVESTING

Table 1 presents the returns from Irish commercial property from 1970 to 2022 and compares them to the returns available from bank deposits. The table also includes Irish inflation statistics.

Table 1: Irish Commercial Property *vs* Bank Deposits *vs* Inflation (compound *p.a.* returns %)

Decade	Irish Commercial Property	Irish 3-month Bank Deposits	Irish Inflation
1970s	17.1	9.6	13.1
1980s	10.5	13.1	8.7
1990s	14.7	7.7	2.4
2000s	4.8	3.2	2.7
2010s	10.1	0.3	0.7
2020s	0.5	0.2	4.2
1970 - 2022	10.7	6.3	5.4

Source: DataStream, FRED, CSO & GillenMarkets.

From 1970-2022, Irish commercial property has generated total returns of 10.7% compound *per annum*. A €10,000 investment would, over that time period, have turned into over €2.2 million. Returns were positive across each decade, although not in every year. Commercial property returns were negative in 11 out of the 53 periods observed, or 21% of the time.

The table also highlights that returns from Irish commercial property were significantly ahead of returns on bank deposits. Bank deposits produced returns of 6.3% compound *per annum*, underperforming commercial property by 5.2% annually. Of course, bank deposit returns were less volatile, and didn't produce a negative return in any year. Returns from Irish commercial property were superior to those from bank deposits in every decade bar the 1980s.

Finally, the table highlights that returns from Irish commercial property have been consistently higher than inflation, which has increased by 5.4% annually since 1970. In other words, Irish commercial property produced positive real (*i.e.*, after inflation) returns of 5.1% compound *per annum*. Only in the most recent decade has inflation exceeded returns from Irish commercial property, although we note that this only covers the 2020-2022 period.

Altogether, the data shows that Irish commercial property has delivered attractive total returns over time, in excess of both bank deposits and inflation.

3: THE THREE DRIVERS OF PROPERTY RETURNS

INITIAL RENTAL YIELD

Initial rental yield is the first component of property returns, and the most intuitive one – when you own a property and rent it to a tenant, they pay you an income in return.

The yield on a property is found by dividing the rental income by the value of the property. For example, a property worth €100,000 that can generate annual rental income of €5,000 has a rental yield of 5.0% (5,000 / 100,000).

Of course, a property investor would be unlikely to keep all of that €5,000 of rental income. Maintenance costs, estate agent fees, and taxes will absorb some of the income. Furthermore, the property may be vacant for some portion of the year if one tenant leaves and another needs to be found.

Therefore, we can distinguish between two types of rental yield: the gross rental yield, which is the 5.0% cited above, and the net rental yield, which accounts for the various costs associated with owning and operating a property.

GROWTH IN THE RENTAL YIELD (INCOME)

The second driver of property returns is growth in the initial rental yield, or rental income. The €5,000 in rental income in the previous section can be reasonably expected to grow over time.

Why might this be the case? **Chart 5** shows the link between US incomes and rental expenditure *per capita* in the US. We use US data as it is available in greater detail and for longer back in history, but the relationship should hold across countries.

Chart 5: US Incomes vs Rent Expenditure *per capita*

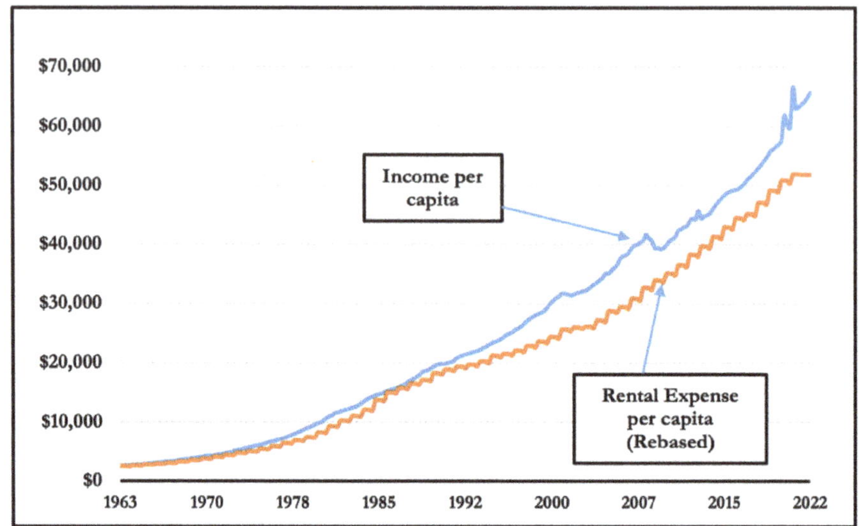

Source: US Census Bureau, US Department of Housing & Urban Development, US Bureau of Economic Analysis, World Bank & Federal Reserve Bank of St Louis.

The chart shows that rental expenditures tend to increase – over long periods of time – in line with incomes. This link makes intuitive sense: rising incomes in society means that workers can afford to pay more in rent (and increases the pool of people that can afford to rent), which should push up rental prices in line with income gains. It is the same rationale behind the link between incomes and property prices. Increasing prosperity means citizens can afford to pay more for property and rent.

The link between rental income and wage growth is not perfect. Governments may, for example, interfere in housing markets by imposing rental caps. Or, more pertinently for Irish investors, supply-demand factors may affect the overall level of rents, if housing is scarce or plentiful.

There may also be idiosyncratic factors at play in individual properties. An investor may, for example, buy a property in a location that is becoming more popular, so that rental income grows faster than overall *per capita* incomes.

However, in general and over time, this rule should hold: rental incomes should increase in line with *per capita* incomes.

UNDERSTANDING WHY INTEREST RATES IMPACT PROPERTY VALUES

Homebuyers & Mortgage Rates

In the section **"The Link Between Income & Property Prices"**, we showed that there is a link between property prices and incomes – as societies become more prosperous, the price of property tends to follow incomes.

However, incomes are not the only determinant of property prices. The second fundamental factor is interest rates, although over a sufficiently long period of time, we expect the key driver of property values to be the initial rental yield and growth in rents.

We can demonstrate this by way of an example. ***Table 2*** shows the affordability of a mortgage under two different scenarios.

Table 2: Mortgage Affordability

Variable	5% rates	2% rates
Income (monthly)	€6,500	€6,500
Deposit	20%	20%
Repayment years	25	25
Mortgage rate	5%	2%
Maximum home value	€347,000	€479,000
Monthly repayment	€1,625	€1,625
Debt service ratio	25%	25%

Source: CSO & GillenMarkets.

A couple is looking to buy their first home. Per the CSO's *Survey on Income & Living Conditions*, the average disposable (post-tax) income for a household with two working people is €78,500, which gives them a combined monthly after-tax income of *circa* €6,500. They have managed to save up a 20% deposit (lucky them!) and are looking for a 25-year mortgage. In order to be comfortable, they would like to limit their mortgage payments to a maximum of 25% of their monthly income (a debt service ratio of 25%).

They want to know, what is the highest price they can pay for a home while satisfying these criteria?

The answer depends on what mortgage interest rate they are offered. Under the scenario of 5% mortgage rates, the maximum home value that they could afford would be €347,000, as the monthly repayment for such a loan would be €1,625, or 25% of their €6,500 monthly income.

Imagine if, while they are viewing potential homes, mortgage rates drop from 5% to 2% – what happens to their affordability then? Because the interest component of their repayments has fallen, they can afford to pay more for a home. With mortgage rates at 2%, the couple could afford to pay up to €479,000 for a home and still maintain their mortgage payments at €1,625 – in other words, they can afford to pay 38% more because of the fall in mortgage rates.

This is a key insight: lower interest rates support higher asset prices. Of course, the corollary is also true: higher interest rates support lower house prices.

Property Investors & Interest Rates

The idea that interest rates impact property (asset) values holds, not just for homeowners, but also for property investors who are looking to generate an income (profit) from their investment.

Imagine that you own a property that generates €50,000 in rental income each year. You would like to retire in five years' time and, at that point, sell your property in order to diversify your investments. You think you can sell the property at the end of year 5 for €625,000. How much is that property worth to you today?

Let's assume that interest rates are 5% over the five-year period. You will receive €50,000 in Years 1 to 4 and €675,000 in Year 5. In total, you will receive €875,000 over the next five years – but the value of the property to you is not €875,000 today. Why so?

Ask yourself, what sum(s) would you need to place in bank deposits today to compound to €875,000 in five years' time (assuming 5% interest rates on bank deposits)? **Table 3** shows that the answer is €706,178 based on the cashflows outlined. For example, €47,619 placed on deposit today becomes €50,000 in one year's time; €45,351 placed on deposit today becomes €50,000 in two years' time – and so forth.

Table 3: Valuing a Property – 1

Year	Cash flows	5% interest rate
1	€50,000	€47,619
2	€50,000	€45,351
3	€50,000	€43,192
4	€50,000	€41,135
5	€675,000	€528,880
Total	**€875,000**	**€706,178**

Source: GillenMarkets.

Pursuing this line of reasoning further, we can demonstrate the effect of lower interest rates on property values. The same property with the same cash flows and sales price will, with 2% interest rates, be worth €801,755 (***Table 4***) – some 14% above the valuation when interest rates were at 5%.

Table 4: Valuing a Property – 2

Year	Cash flows	2% interest rate
1	€50,000	€49,020
2	€50,000	€48,058
3	€50,000	€47,116
4	€50,000	€46,192
5	€675,000	€611,368
Total	**€875,000**	**€801,755**

Source: GillenMarkets

In the previous example, €47,619 placed on deposit became €50,000 in one year. In this new era of 2% interest rates, €49,020 is needed to achieve €50,000 in one year.

As with the example of the homebuyers, the central insight is the same: lower interest rates support higher property prices, and higher interest rates imply lower property prices.

This insight can be intuited if one considers asset classes being in competition with each other for scarce capital. In an environment of 5% interest rates, the maximum price at which you would value the property is

€706,178 – any higher, and the return earned would be less than bank deposits. Since property is a risk asset, the return it offers should *at least* match the return available from bank deposits – and preferably exceed it.

If interest rates then decline to 2%, suddenly the 5% available from your property becomes much more attractive – and buyers will bid the price up to reflect the increased attractiveness relative to bank deposits.

(Note that, in the above example, we have ignored for the sake of simplicity the idea of a risk premium, and also assumed that the sales price of the property in **Table 4** doesn't move even as interest rates fall.)

4: THE MAJOR RISKS IN PROPERTY INVESTING

There are three key risks in property investing: the location risks; the financial risks; and the valuation risks.

If you have read any of our research notes before, this framework should appear familiar to you. We always categorise the risks of investing in businesses as: the business risks; the financial risks; and the valuation risks.

LOCATION RISK

As the saying goes, the three most important things in real estate are "location, location, location!"

To put a finer point on it, location risk is a broad bucket which describes the possibility that the rental income from a property investment, and/or asset values, declines as a result of some impairment to the property.

As with businesses, impairment can occur as a result of myriad factors. For residential properties, perhaps the area in which the property resides becomes a less desirable area in which to live. Or perhaps some structural defect is found in the property that requires significant investment to repair. For example, the "Mica scandal" in Donegal exposed many property owners to significant repair liabilities before the government stepped in with the Defective Concrete Blocks Grant Scheme.

For commercial properties, the usefulness of the building to businesses may decline over time – London skyscrapers, for example, are facing a difficult period as the advent of work-from-home practices appear to be permanently reducing demand for central office space. If this trend continues, it is, in effect, a permanent reduction of rental income for the owner of those properties. Or a tenant may become financially challenged and unable to pay rent on time or in full. Many retailers, challenged by the rise of online retail, have seen sales levels decline precipitously, which has put their business models under pressure and reduced the amount of cash flows available to pay rent on properties.

FINANCIAL RISK

Financial risk arises through the use of inappropriate financing and/or excessive debt levels.

A borrower who can no longer pay down their debt or satisfy their interest payments may see their property seized by the lender and disposed of. In a worst-case scenario, there is no guarantee that the proceeds returned following the sale – after the lender's loan has been repaid – will be equal to the amount of capital invested by the borrower in the property. The more debt an investor uses to finance the purchase of a property, the lower the margin of safety they have against adverse developments.

In other words, if you bought a property with debt and funded a portion of the investment yourself (the equity), you could lose the equity in a bankruptcy process.

VALUATION RISK

Valuation risk occurs when an investor overpays for an asset, which reduces the future returns, perhaps to very low levels. One of the (many) issues that contributed to the Irish financial crisis in 2007-08 was the excessive valuation placed on properties at that time. At the height of the property bubble in Ireland, residential properties were trading at 8.3 times the national average income – compared to a long-term average of 4.7 times.

While there were many issues at play in the financial crisis, it is undeniable that investors overpaying for property contributed significantly to, and magnified, the subsequent losses.

MULTIPLYING RISKS

While each of the above risks can be experienced in isolation, experiencing them together can exacerbate losses. We can imagine a nightmare scenario as an example. An investor buys a retail property at a high valuation and finances the investment with debt. Subsequently, the central bank raises interest rates to cool the economy, thus pushing the economy into recession.

The investor would possibly be faced with a triple whammy – declining rental income as the retailer's sales shrink, higher interest payments on the debt, and a falling valuation. This is the type of scenario in which one's entire capital could be wiped out.

But of course, there is no need to imagine these scenarios. Real life abounds with examples of risks interacting with, and multiplying, each other. For example, we mentioned in the last section that investors were paying stretched valuations for Irish houses in the 2003 to 2007 period. This risk was then compounded by the use of a mortgage to finance these investments. When the Irish housing market subsequently crashed, investors were left paying mortgages on significantly devalued properties, a situation known as "negative equity".

5: GAINING EXPOSURE TO PROPERTY

There are three main ways to invest in property: purchase a property directly ("physical property investing"), unlisted investment funds, and listed property funds and companies.

PHYSICAL PROPERTY

For retail investors in Ireland, this is likely the most common way to gain exposure to property as an asset class. Exposure will typically be through residential properties, as the capital required to invest in commercial properties is higher.

There is a perception among Irish retail investors that direct property investing is less risky than listed property funds or companies. This is likely because direct property does not come with a daily price quotation, and so the investor is not subjected to the emotions of daily stock gyrations. This is, however, a fallacy – the value of a direct property investment changes just as much and as frequently as the value of listed equities. Yes, property may be less volatile than listed equities, but the risks embedded in both asset types are the same.

In our view, investing in direct property is often *more* risky than investing through listed or unlisted funds. To purchase a direct property, an investor must buy in a single place (location risk), likely financing a large part of the purchase with a mortgage (financial risk), and at a single point in time (increasing valuation risk – *i.e.*, the risk that you buy when property prices offer poor value).

Tax treatment of physical property

Rental income is subject to income tax at your marginal rate. Capital gains are taxed at a 33% rate and losses can be offset against capital gains elsewhere.

INVESTMENT FUNDS (UNLISTED)

An unlisted fund is typically an open-ended investment vehicle which pools together investors' capital to invest in a particular asset class. The term 'open-ended' means that an investor can sell ('redeem') their shares or units back to the fund at net asset value. The ability to redeem shares at net asset value can be an attractive feature of this type of fund. The frequency with which an investor can redeem their shares in the fund varies from daily to longer periods of time (*e.g.,* quarterly).

There are many unlisted funds in Ireland. The following is a non-exhaustive list of the major property investment funds: Davy Irish Property Fund, Irish Life Irish Property Fund, Aviva Irish Commercial Property Fund, IPUT, Gresham House Commercial Property Fund, Zurich Life Property Fund. In some cases, these funds are Qualifying Investor Alternative Investment Funds (QIAIFs), meaning that investors must demonstrate knowledge of investing and commit to a minimum investment of €100,000.

The majority of property investment funds focus on commercial property.

The main advantages of investing in property through funds, as opposed to directly in a physical property, are the following:

- An investor gains exposure to a diversified portfolio, dealing with location risk;

- The fund may employ some gearing, but the investor is not personally liable for it, and the gearing levels of a property fund are typically lower than for direct property investments, thus lowering financial risk;

- The investor can build an investment with small monthly contributions, brick by brick, allowing the investor to average in over time, thus lowering valuation risk.

In addition to dealing with the three key risks – location, financial, valuation – investors in property funds also gain access to professional management teams, who know how to assess values and manage property investments, and deal with the day-to-day problems that arise.

The key drawback of open-ended funds investing in illiquid assets is the regular liquidity that investors are entitled to. Most of the time, an open-ended fund is unlikely to experience large (net) redemption requests, so can keep a small amount of cash or a credit facility available to meet redemptions.

However, if an open-ended fund receives a large amount of redemption requests at once, it can be forced to sell assets (often at a discount) or to suspend redemptions, leaving investors facing either a permanent, potentially large loss, or the prospect of having no way to access their capital until the fund is reopened for redemptions.

Open-ended funds that invest in illiquid assets have encountered this issue reasonably frequently in the past, so this risk is not simply a theoretical one, and tends to occur during periods of market stress.

Tax treatment of unlisted investment funds

Income and gains accumulate tax-free within the fund. Investors are subject to the gains tax rate (41%) upon disposal, or after a period of eight years has elapsed (the "deemed disposal" rule). There is no loss relief available unless the investor is switching between funds under the same legal umbrella fund structure.

LISTED PROPERTY FUNDS & STOCKS

Investors can gain access to property through investment funds (investment trusts, real estate investment trusts and exchange-traded funds) and companies that are listed on the stock market.

Listed investment trusts are closed-ended funds that raise capital through initial public offerings and then list on the stock market. A shareholder in a closed-ended fund cannot sell their shares back to the fund, and instead must find another buyer for the shares in the market. Because the share price is divorced from the value of the underlying portfolio (or net asset value), it can trade above (a premium) or below (a discount) the net asset value. This feature of closed-ended funds represents both a downside and an upside of the structure, with the upside being that buying the shares of an investment trust at a discount to net asset value allows the investor to potentially earn two sources of return: net asset value growth, and additional returns from the narrowing of a discount that may have opened up.

Because the manager is not required to redeem shareholders' investments at net asset value, closed-ended funds are much better suited to investing in illiquid assets like private equity or property.

In many cases, stock market-listed property companies can avail of real estate investment trust (REIT) legislation, which exists in many countries. In Ireland, for example, a REIT that distributes 85% of its income to shareholders (among other requirements) can avoid paying capital gains or corporation tax. This tax is levied on individual shareholders, thus avoiding double taxation.

For GillenMarkets' clients and subscribers, we cover two main listed property funds:

- Irish Residential Properties REIT, which owns a portfolio of *circa* 4,000 apartments primarily in Dublin and the surrounding regions; and

- TR Property Trust, a London-listed investment trust that invests in the shares of listed European property companies and a small amount of direct UK property. We provide profiles of these companies at the end of this booklet.

Tax treatment of REITs, investment trusts & listed property companies

The treatment of dividend income will depend on the location of the dividend paid. While investment trusts are not specifically dealt with by the Irish Revenue, the existence of REIT legislation in Ireland suggests that the two structures should be treated similarly.

- **Irish shares:** A 25% withholding tax is applied. 100% of the dividend is assessable for income tax purposes, and the 25% withheld tax is deemed to be tax paid. For pension accounts, the dividend can be paid without the withholding tax, or it can be reclaimed.

- **UK shares:** No withholding tax is applied by the UK taxation authorities. Dividend income received is subject to tax at your marginal rate of income tax in Ireland.

- **US shares:** A 30% withholding tax is applied, unless a W-8BEN form is filed, in which case the rate is reduced to 15%. 100% of the dividend is assessable for income tax purposes in Ireland, and the 15% withheld is deemed to be tax already paid. For pension accounts, the 15% withholding tax is non-refundable.

- **Shares from other OECD countries:** In general, double taxation treaties allow the source country (where the dividend is paid from) to apply a withholding tax, which is then treated as tax already paid in Ireland.

Capital gains in REITs, investment trusts, and companies are subject to a 33% capital gains tax rate and losses can be offset against gains elsewhere.

Exchange-traded Funds (ETFs)

Investors can also gain access to property through exchange-traded funds (ETFs), which passively replicate the performance of an index of property companies. ETFs provide broad, diversified exposure to property companies, each of which owns a portfolio of individual properties and are typically cheaper than actively managed property investment funds. They also mitigate the three key risks, and investors get the benefit of professional management through the property companies/funds that the ETF invests in. We provide profiles of two property-focused ETFs at the end of this booklet.

Tax treatment of ETFs

ETFs domiciled within the EU and subject to UCITS regulations are taxed in the same way as unlisted funds. Income and gains can accumulate tax-free within the fund. Investors are subject to a gains tax rate (41%) upon disposal, or after a period of eight years has elapsed (the "deemed disposal" rule). There is no loss relief available – *i.e.*, losses on one ETF cannot be used against gains elsewhere.

PHYSICAL PROPERTY – THE EXAMPLE OF IRES REIT

We stated in the "**Physical Property**" section that investing in direct properties can be riskier than through property funds or stocks. A bold claim! We can elaborate by way of an example.

IRES REIT, the largest landlord in Ireland, is a real estate investment trust listed on the Irish Stock Exchange. It has seen its share price fall from a peak of €1.83 back in December 2019 to €1.11 at the end of December 2022. At that price, the shares traded at a 34% discount to the actual market value of its 4,000 rented apartments portfolio of €1.68 a share.

So, what's up?

Because IRES REIT's shares trade on the stock exchange, the share price can decouple from the trust's net asset value when there is an excess of sellers – as is currently the case. We can see three separate risks that are likely worrying investors.

First up is the company's debt, which represents 43% of its assets. Its interest bill is already rising as the ECB raises interest rates. Along with rising interest rates, operating costs are increasing, and rental growth is capped in Dublin, thus putting pressure on earnings (and the dividend).

Next up is political risk. And it's not insignificant. Should Sinn Féin win the next election, who knows what draconian policies they could adopt in an attempt to control rents and make housing more affordable.

And thirdly, rising interest rates and rising unemployment can be expected to at least soften up property prices in the capital given that they are at significantly elevated levels relative to incomes.

Against a backdrop of rising interest rates, property and share prices often fall in order to offer a higher yield (return), which then enables them to continue to attract investor interest.

So, investors in Irish property listed on the stock market are simply looking forward. These three likely concerns may or may not come to pass, but that's what the market does. It anticipates possible risks.

Chart 6: IRES REIT – Share Price *vs* NAV

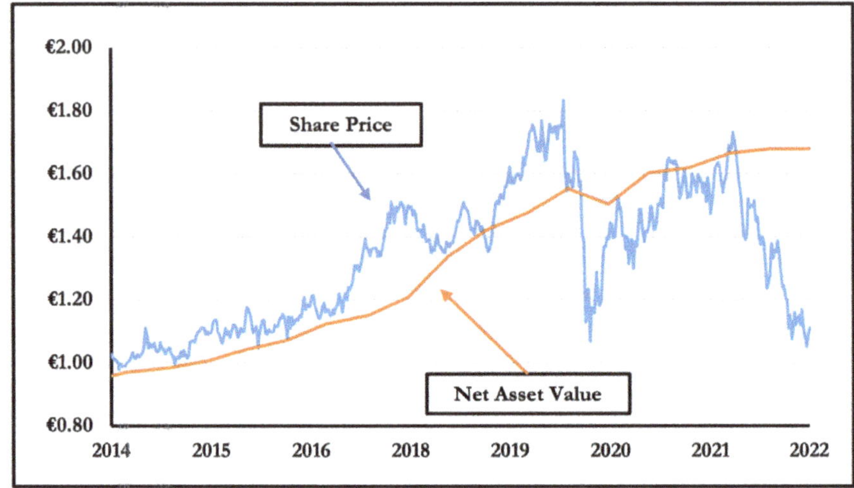

Source: Bloomberg.

What does this have to do with investing directly in property?

From an investment perspective, the risks in IRES REIT's property portfolio and rental income stream are exactly the same as the risks faced by all investors that directly own apartments in Dublin.

The majority of people who own an apartment for investment purposes probably have a mortgage (debt) and many will mostly have a higher proportion of debt against the property compared to IRES REIT. They are also likely to have floating rate debt, so that their interest bill is already rising.

And they own property at similar valuations to IRES REIT, so that they have the same valuation risk as IRES REIT and investors in IRES REIT shares.

The person with cash to invest today, of course, now has a choice. They can buy a single apartment as an investment at elevated valuations in a single location with debt getting more costly and faced with the same political risks.

Or they can buy IRES REIT's shares, which offer far better diversification (4,000 apartments compared to one) and have already discounted some of the aforementioned risks by 34%. And they can invest as little or as much as they wish and without the need to use any debt.

The point isn't that IRES REIT is risk-free just because its shares look cheap *versus* the alternative of buying a physical property. Rather, we are trying to dispel the notion that investing in physical property is *less* risky than investing in property through funds or the stock market.

The risks faced by an investor are the same in both cases. Indeed, investing directly in physical property usually requires more debt, and often heightens both valuation and location risks. These risks are much more easily controlled by investing through listed or unlisted funds and stocks.

Determining whether you are a lump-sum or regular investor is a key part of the investment journey.

We define a lump-sum investor as one who has a single sum of capital to invest and is unlikely to add meaningfully to that lump-sum over time. (*e.g.,* by earning an income). The lump-sum investor can invest in the market once or can drip-feed in sums over time.

A regular investor is one with a regular income stream that can invest into markets regularly over long periods of time.

The key difference between the two is valuation risk. A regular investor, because they are investing over periods of years, does not have to overly worry about the timing of their investment. In some months or years, values (prices) may be poor, and in others values will be much better. On average and over a long period of time, the regular investor will most likely get a fair price for their investment.

The lump-sum investor, however, only gets a few bites at the cherry. Even if the lump-sum investor decides to drip-feed monies into the market, they likely can't do this for as long as the regular investor. As such, the risk of overpaying for an asset is higher, which can reduce subsequent returns. Greater attention must be paid by the lump-sum investor to the value obtained (price paid).

PHYSICAL PROPERTY

It is very difficult for a regular investor to invest in physical property – at least, without the use of debt. To build a direct property portfolio 'brick by brick' is all but impossible for the regular investor.

A lump-sum investor can, depending on the amount of money, purchase a property directly without the use of debt.

As we have made clear in **"The Major Risks in Property Investing"**, direct property investing is not without risk – but this is not to say that we are against it entirely. Where the risks are controlled properly, direct property can be an attractive asset which should, over time, provide an income stream that grows in line with society's prosperity. However, the perception that it is less risky than investing in listed or unlisted funds is incorrect.

STOCKS & FUNDS

It is much easier for the regular investor to build a brick-by-brick property portfolio through property funds, be they unlisted funds or stock market-listed funds or property companies. For example, a regular investor could invest €1,000 a month into a property fund, and, over time, they would build a diversified portfolio of properties, without the use of debt, while also benefitting from professional property management and the judgment of a fund manager who is paid to assess where the best value lies.

A lump-sum investor can also easily invest in property through property funds (listed or unlisted) and property companies. As we stated previously, valuation risk must be properly assessed, to avoid overpaying for assets, which inevitably reduces the subsequent returns. A professional manager at TR Property Trust or Irish Residential Properties REIT is capable of judging the value on offer but, in the case where an entire asset class becomes overvalued, investors are still subject to valuation risk. As such, careful attention must be paid when deciding to invest.

LUMP-SUM *vs* REGULAR INVESTING: AN EXAMPLE

We can show how lump-sum and regular investors differ by way of example. (Note: We ignore taxes in both cases to make matters simpler.)

We begin our example in April 2007, the peak of the Irish residential property market. For the **regular investor**, they begin a €1,867 monthly investment programme. (This may seem high: it is done simply to make the figures between the regular investor and lump-sum investor comparable.[1]) The money is invested in shares of TR Property Trust, a London-listed investment trust that invests in listed property companies in the UK and Europe. We assume that the dividend income accumulates in the share-dealing account in cash.

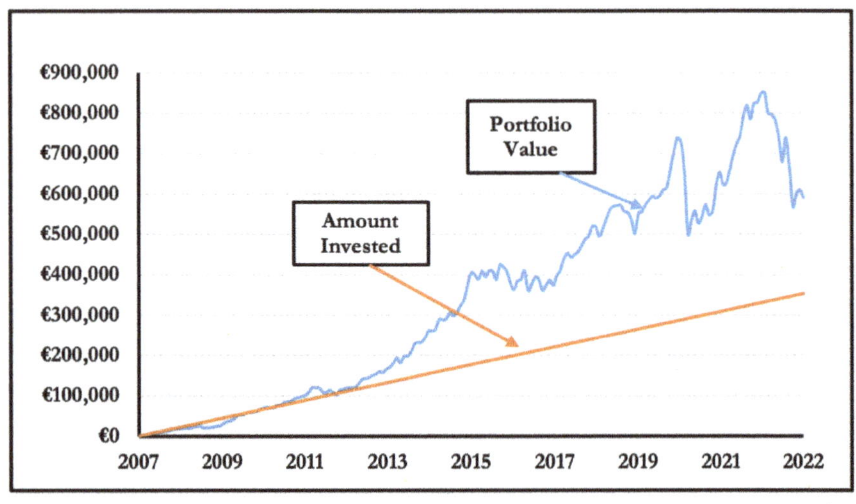

Chart 7: Regular Investing in TR Property

Source: Bloomberg & GillenMarkets.

Chart 7 shows the outcome for our regular investor. They were more or less immediately underwater (*i.e.*, the portfolio value was less than the amount invested), and remained so until February 2010, almost three years later. In total, the portfolio was underwater for 34 months, or 18% of the time.

By December 2022, after 189 months of the programme, the regular investor had contributed €353,000 to their property portfolio, composed entirely of TR Property shares. This portfolio gave them exposure to a diversified collection of European residential and commercial property companies. The market value of this portfolio, including dividends of €154,000,

---

[1]   A €1,867 monthly contribution over 189 months from April 2007 to December 2022 totals €353,000, the same amount invested by the lump-sum investor in April 2007.

was €592,000. This represents a total gain of 68%, or an annualised return of 6.3%.

The **lump-sum investor** also begins their investment journey in April 2007, buying an Irish residential property for *circa* €353,000 (the national average at that date). The property is rented to a tenant, with the income adjusting to market rates every two years. We assume that 20% of the rental income is absorbed by vacancies, letting fees, maintenance costs, etc. We assume that rental income accumulates in the investor's bank account.

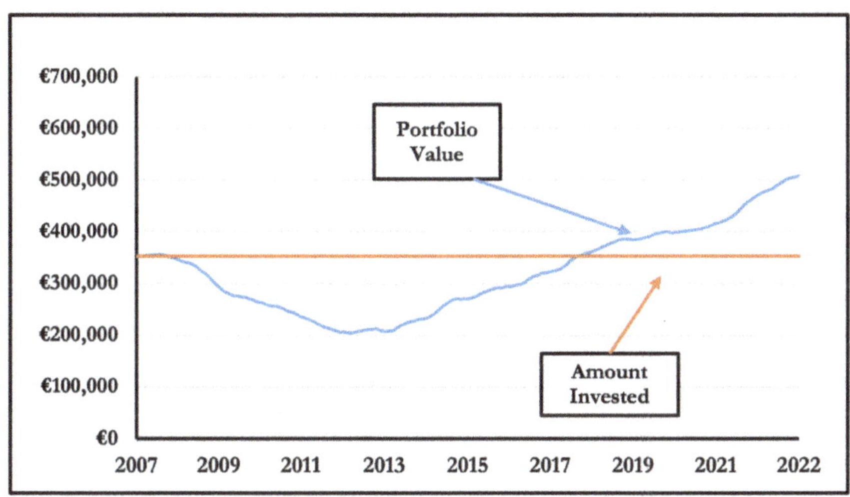

Chart 8: Lump-sum Investor: Irish Property

Source: CSO, Residential Tenancies Board, Bloomberg & GillenMarkets.

Chart 8 shows the outcome for our lump-sum investor. They were underwater after nine months, and remained so until October 2017, over 10 years later. The property price fell 55% from the peak in April 2007 to the trough in March 2013. In total, the portfolio was underwater for 117 months, or 62% of the time.

By December 2022, the total value of the house and accumulated rental income was €509,000, representing a total gain of 44% and an annualised return of 2.8%.

The property price in December 2022 was estimated at €364,500, just 3.2% above the purchase price of €353,000 in April 2007. The majority of the gains came from rental income of €144,000 over the life of the investment.

In sum, it appears clear to us that the regular investor has fared better than the lump-sum investor, with a more rapid recovery from the property crash and more favourable returns over the life of the investment.

Furthermore, the lump-sum investor likely would have had to take out a mortgage to fund part of the property purchase, adding an element of financial risk to the equation. The regular investor, on the other hand, built the portfolio brick-by-brick with savings and without the use of borrowings.

This section highlights the importance, for lump-sum investors, of ensuring that they obtain reasonable value when investing. Imagine the psychic pain of buying an Irish residential property in April 2007 with a mortgage – never mind the paltry subsequent returns!

Quite simply, in Ireland at least, buying overvalued property with a high proportion financed with debt at a single point in time (*i.e.*, the lump-sum investor) anywhere between 2003 and 2007 was a disaster for people's savings and investment (and lives) and inflicted significant personal traumas. It need not have happened had people understood how to invest.

7: FUND PROFILE: IRISH LIFE PROPERTY FUND

Irish Life Irish Property Fund offers investors exposure to Irish commercial property across a spread of office, retail, and industrial assets. The fund has a gross asset value of €1.8 billion and holds 69 assets.

Summary Information	
Share price (31-Dec-22)	n/a
NAV per share	€0.27
Market value	n/a
Net assets	€1.5 billion
Ticker code	n/a
ISIN	n/a
Fund type	Open-ended fund
Dividend yield	n/a
Discount/premium	n/a
TER	n/a
Gearing/(net cash)	n/a

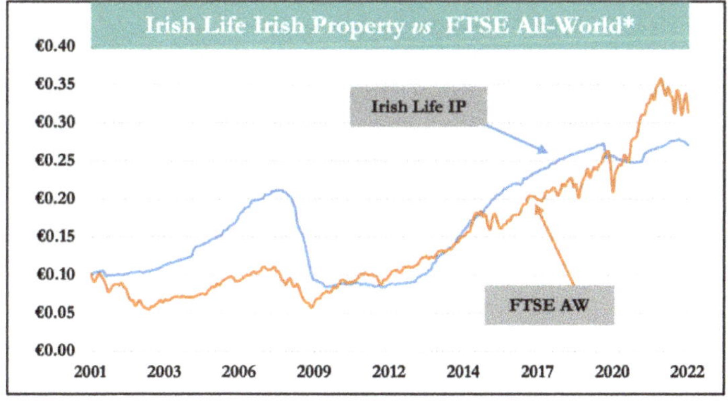

* Total return in euro terms.

8: FUND PROFILE: IRISH RESIDENTIAL PROPERTIES REIT

Irish Residential Properties REIT is an Irish-listed real estate investment trust investing in multi-family residential units (*i.e.*, apartments). Since listing in 2014, the trust has raised €550 million in equity capital, which it has invested in a high-quality portfolio of *circa* 4,000 apartments located primarily in the Dublin region.

Summary Information	
Share price (31-Dec-22)	€1.11
NAV per share	€1.68
Market value	€588 million
Net assets	€889 million
Ticker code	IRES ID
ISIN	IE00BJ34P519
Fund type	Closed-ended Fund
Dividend yield	4.6%
Discount/premium	-33.8%
TER	1.70%
Gearing/(net cash)	42.6%

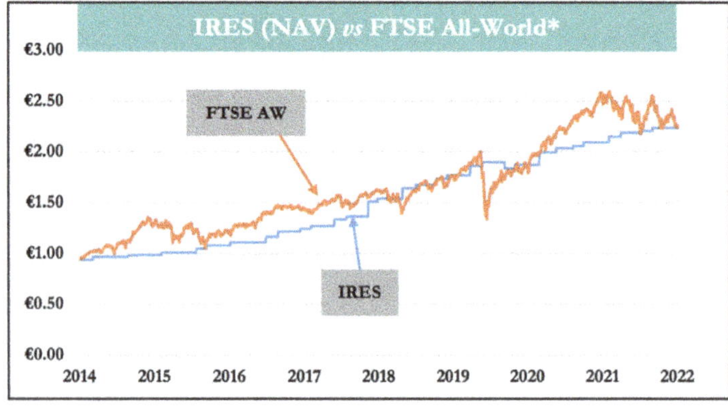

** Total return in euro terms.*

9: FUND PROFILE: iSHARES DEVELOPED MARKETS PROPERTY YIELD ETF

The iShares Developed Markets Property Yield ETF offers exposure to listed real estate companies and trusts in developed countries. It tracks the FTSE EPRA/NAREIT Developed Dividend+ Index, which only includes companies trading on a forecast dividend yield of at least 2%, and trades on multiple European exchanges in EUR, GBP and USD.

Summary Information	
Share price (31-Dec-22)	€20.81
NAV per share	€20.81
Market value	€1,507 million
Net assets	€1,507 million
Ticker code	IWDP NA
ISIN	IE00B1FZS350
Fund type	Exchange-traded fund
Dividend yield	3.6%
Discount/premium	n/a
TER	0.59%
Gearing/(net cash)	n/a

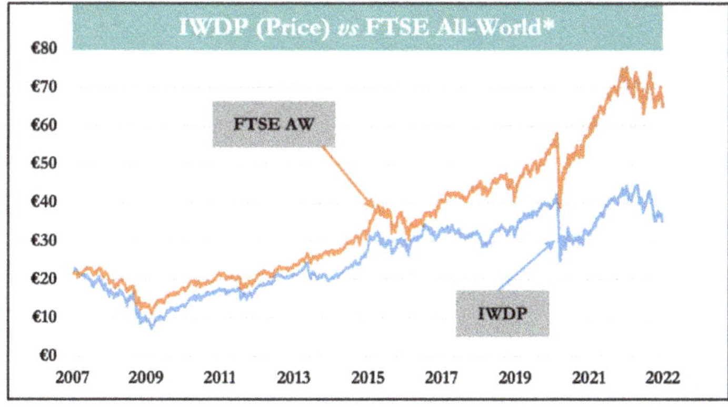

Total return in euro terms.

10: FUND PROFILE: iSHARES EUROPEAN PROPERTY YIELD ETF

The iShares European Property Yield ETF offers exposure to listed real estate companies and trusts in developed European companies (excluding the UK). It tracks the FTSE EPRA/NAREIT Developed Europe ex-UK Dividend+ Index, which only includes companies trading on a forecast dividend yield of at least 2%, and trades on multiple European exchanges in EUR and GBP.

Summary Information	
Share price (31-Dec-22)	€25.93
NAV per share	€25.93
Market value	€1,152 million
Net assets	€1,152 million
Ticker code	IPRP NA
ISIN	IE00B0M63284
Fund type	Exchange-traded Fund
Dividend yield	4.1%
Discount/premium	n/a
TER	0.40%
Gearing/(net cash)	n/a

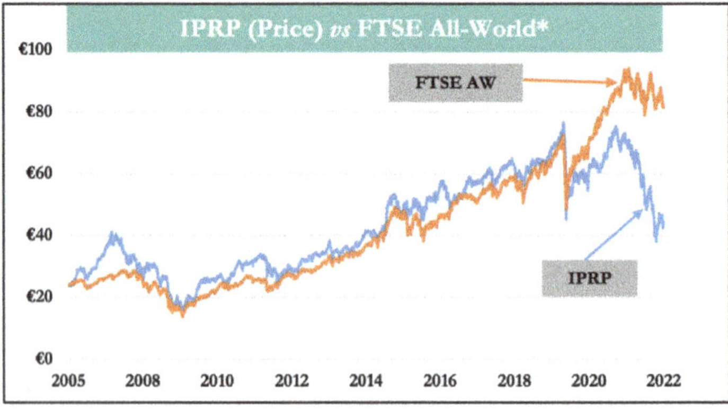

Total return in euro terms.

11: FUND PROFILE: TR PROPERTY INVESTMENT TRUST

TR Property Trust is a London-listed investment trust that aims to generate capital and income growth for shareholders by investing in the securities of property companies and trusts listed in the UK and continental Europe. The trust also offers a small amount of exposure to direct UK property.

Summary Information	
Share price (31-Dec-22)	£3.06
NAV per share	£3.27
Market value	£970 million
Net assets	£1,038 million
Ticker code	TRY LN
ISIN	GB0009064097
Fund type	Closed-ended Fund
Dividend yield	4.9%
Discount/premium	-6.6%
TER	0.81%
Gearing/(net cash)	14%

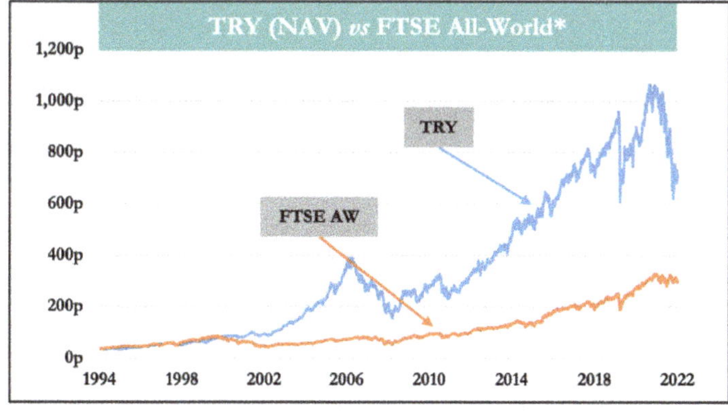

* Total return in GBP terms.

GLOSSARY

Exchange-Traded Fund (ETF): A fund listed on a stock exchange, which can be bought or sold like shares in companies or trusts. Exchange-traded funds are structured so that the net asset value of the underlying portfolio does not deviate significantly from the ETF's share price. ETFs can invest in a variety of asset classes – equities, bonds, commodities – and are often passively managed, meaning they track the performance of an underlying index. ETFs are popular for their low-cost and for the ease with which they allow investors to diversify their portfolios.

Government Bonds: Securities issued by governments to fund state expenditure. In return for an investor's capital, the government promises to make timely payments of interest and guarantees the return of the investor's capital when the bond matures. Government bonds are often available to be bought in the marketplace, so the market price of a bond can differ from the price at which at which it was issued. 'Coupon' is the term used to refer to the interest payment a bondholder receives. Coupons are used to determine the bond's interest rate. For example, a €5 annual coupon on a bond with a price of €100 equates to an interest rate of 5% (5 / 100). If the price of the bond moved up to, say, €105 due to increased demand in the market, the interest rate would fall to 4.8%. In other words, falling interest rates imply higher bond prices. The reverse is also true – rising interest rates imply lower bond prices.

Property Investment Company: A broad term used to describe a company which invests in property. Typically, a property investment company will own rental properties, and will also undertake development activity to construct new properties that can be added to its portfolio of rental properties upon completion.

Real Estate Investment Trust (REIT): Real estate investment trusts (REITs) are investment companies which, when in compliance with relevant legislation, are exempt from capital gains and income tax. Income and capital gains are taxed, instead, in the hands of shareholders. In Ireland, the key requirement is that 85% of income must be paid out to shareholders each year. Four REITs have listed in Ireland since legislation was introduced in 2013, but three have since been acquired (Hibernia REIT, Green REIT, Yew Grove REIT) and thus delisted. The sole remaining listed REIT is Irish Residential Properties REIT.

Rental Yield: The rental yield on a property is defined as the annual rental income divided by the value of the property. So, for example, a property worth €100,000 that can generate annual rental income of €5,000 has a rental yield of 5.0% (5,000 / 100,000). Of course, a property investor would be unlikely to keep all of that €5,000 of rental income. Maintenance costs, estate agent fees, and taxes will absorb some of the income. Furthermore, the property may be vacant for some portion of the year if one tenant leaves and another needs to be found. Therefore, we can distinguish between two types of rental yield: the gross rental yield, which is the 5.0% cited above, and the net rental yield, which accounts for the various costs associated with owning and operating a property.

Shares: A share (used interchangeably with 'equities' and 'stocks') entitles its owner ('shareholder') to a proportionate share of a company's profits after all other stakeholders have been paid. Shares can be both unlisted (private equity) or listed (public equity). Because shareholders are paid last after all other creditors, it is the riskiest asset class to own. This explains why, historically, equities as an asset class have tended to generate the highest returns over long periods of time – and also the highest volatility.

Bricks & Mortar through Stocks & Shares

This booklet was written by Darren Gillen, research analyst at GillenMarkets, and is aimed at the reader who is interested in learning about the various ways to invest in property.

Buying a property is a common way for retail investors to invest their savings, and this is particularly the case in Ireland. Bricks and mortar are tangible and easily understood, while the stock market appears to many to be mystifying and volatile.

As is often the case in investing, misconceptions abound. Direct property investing is riskier than many assume, and property investing through the stock market is less risky than popular perceptions would have you believe.

This booklet aims to give you a more nuanced understanding of property investing, the key drivers of returns and how to invest in property through the stock market. A sound plan for investing in property that mitigates the key risks is the ticket to attractive returns. We hope that this booklet serves as a reliable guide in that regard.

Gillen.

E: info@gillenmarkets.com
T: +353 1 2871400
W: www.gillenmarkets.com